HOW TO BUILD A GLOBAL SUPPLY CHAIN FOR YOUR BUSINESS

A GUIDE FOR NEW AND EXPERIENCED PROFESSIONALS ON HOW TO "GO GLOBAL" WITH YOUR SUPPLY CHAIN

DISCLAIMER

No part of this book can be transmitted or reproduced in any form, including print, electronic, photocopying, scanning, mechanical, or recording without prior written permission from the author.

This is a work of creative nonfiction. The guidelines are portrayed to the best of the author's intuition and experience. While all the information in this book is true, some names and identifying details have been changed to protect the privacy of the people involved.

This book has been written for information purposes only. Every effort has been made to make this book as complete and accurate as possible. However, there may be mistakes in typography or content. Also, this book provides information only up to the publishing date, so it may not include some information about the author's business experience.

The author and the publisher do not warrant that the information contained in this book is fully complete and shall not be responsible for any errors or omissions. The author and publisher shall have neither liability nor responsibility to any person or entity with respect to any loss or damage caused or alleged to be caused directly or indirectly by this book.

ISBN: 978-0-578-95343-4

TABLE OF CONTENTS

A GUIDE FOR NEW AND EXPERIENCED PROFESSIONALS ON HOW TO "GO GLOBAL" WITH YOUR SUPPLY CHAIN

About the Author

Sergio Retamal is the CEO of Global4PL, a supply chain operations and consulting services company that helps organizations increase international sales, improve compliance, and achieve their full operational potential. Global4PL provides IOR-EOR services in over 168 countries, technology solutions, and supply chain consulting services. Sergio's career spans over 25 years in procurement and supply chain management. His professional experience includes management roles in the United States, Asia, Europe, and Latin America.

About the Book

This book is a guide to become a US-based exporter. It goes into great detail, depicting the various types of situations that could result in problems in the world of exporting. It further describes how you can overcome those problems.

This book is a one-go manifesto on how to become a proficient exporter and the complete guide you need to step a foot in the world of exporting. If you are inclined to become an exporter but you don't know where to start, Sergio Retamal has got your back. Even those who already know how to export and are already there in the industry can find valuable lessons in this short but powerful book.

HOW TO BUILD A GLOBAL SUPPLY CHAIN FOR YOUR BUSINESS

A GUIDE FOR NEW AND EXPERIENCED PROFESSIONALS ON HOW TO "GO GLOBAL" WITH YOUR SUPPLY CHAIN

CHAPTER ONE

INTRODUCTION

A couple of decades ago, logistics would hardly be mentioned in the long-term planning of even the largest companies. Today, the strategic role of the supply chain is recognized by most every organization. We now live in a networked, distributed economy that's global in nature and characterized by dynamic business relationships. No organization, whether a firm, non-profit, or a government entity, can survive on its own. It relies on relationships with other organizations in the contemporary business world. The supply chain refers to a closely connected, supportive network that competes with other networks. The major forces that allow these networks to grow are an expanding reach, and ease of access to IT and communication technology. As the competition intensifies, these factors are becoming essential to every organization's very survival.

Every single day, products reach customers after traveling long routes with numerous business entities involved in production and distribution. For example, a laptop can be designed in the U.S., produced in China, and sent to a consumer in Australia.

While this is only one simple example, the majority of products in most retail stores move through the global supply chain. Furthermore, information technology and communication channels are creating new opportunities. New markets are developing, global trade is expanding, and there's a dramatic focus today on environmental concerns. The global supply chain remains quite responsive to these changes, and plays a vital role in addressing them.

This book builds on the basic principles of supply chain management and takes it to the next level by focusing on how companies can go global. It won't cover every aspect of the supply chain, but will focus on areas of current interest, including how recent changes should be addressed, and how key issues can be resolved.

While there are always gaps between academic knowledge and professional practices, this book attempts to bridge those gaps. Everything mentioned in this book is based on my past international trade experiences: the way I grew my logistics business to a global level and the road I traveled to success. Hence, all the aspects discussed in this book are practical and tested.

As for the target audience, this book is mainly written for the millions of business development gurus and business owners who wish to go global or expand further on a global scale. In addition, this book can provide insight for any supply chain professional or student seeking practical and up-to-date knowledge on this topic.

CHAPTER TWO

THERE ARE MORE CUSTOMERS OUTSIDE THE USA THAN IN THE USA

No matter how small your business, there is plenty of opportunity to start selling goods and services abroad. As of today, a large chunk of U.S. exports are attributed to small and medium-sized businesses. Between 2005 and 2013, a remarkable 28% increase was recorded in the number of small and medium-sized U.S. firms exporting to at least one international market. It's worth noting that 97% of the U.S. exporters today are small business enterprises (SMEs) with less than 500 employees. In fact, 75% of U.S. exporters have less than 20 employees. This helps explain why 7 in 10 new jobs in the U.S. are created by small businesses.

At the same time, digital transformations are compounding this trend at an exponential rate. When you have an Internet presence with a global marketing and order-taking platform, selling beyond international boundaries becomes much easier. To further expand your reach, you can translate the key pages of your company's website into a multitude of languages. With a small investment, you can integrate a payment gateway solution to provide credit card processing for your customers. Thus, you can easily join the game without having to spend too many years in business or investing too much.

With numerous e-commerce solutions to choose from, including various B2B and B2C marketplaces, conducting business across the globe is easier than ever. You can quickly create an appealing virtual storefront and, more importantly, tap into a global army of buyers. In addition to payment solutions, these platforms help you find a shipper who can facilitate the process as well as manage the necessary documentation. Many shippers also offer freight forwarding and customs brokerage services, international business advice, cost calculators, and financing options. It's that easy: your products will be picked up from your location and delivered anywhere in the world.

As your sales increase, some large e-commerce platforms allow you to stock large quantities of your highest selling products at their fulfillment centers. As those items are sold and delivered to customers, you can supply more inventory to the centers. This way, less shipping costs will be incurred for shipping items one-by-one. Order fulfillment efficiencies also improve.

If those sales channels aren't the right fit or your product has a more customized nature, you can consider attending trade shows within the U.S.—either physically or virtually—where potential international buyers visit to purchase U.S. products. Event organizers can also work with government agencies to introduce you to foreign buyers. This service is called customized business matchmaking. Likewise, you might want to attend similar events in other countries, where your country's embassy network will help you generate new business, saving you a lot of time and money. With the help of the same government agencies, you can find buyers and meet customers from more than 100 countries.

Aside from these types of sales channels, there are numerous other options. If you're a small business looking to sell to multiple overseas markets, the global trading system is the perfect one offering multiple marketing and sales channels.

Yet, many U.S. exporters choose to sell to only one overseas market, which is Canada. While small businesses are major contributors to U.S. exports, the majority of those firms do not sell to more than one country. Indeed, the smaller the company, the less likely it is to sell to more than one country. There are many reasons that small business owners choose not to expand beyond international boundaries. Let's explore some of these reasons.

THERE IS NO NEED TO FEAR EXPORTING, IF YOU DO IT RIGHT

The main reason most small companies don't export more is fear of the unknown. For an American businessperson, exporting to Canada is perceived as less risky than selling to India or Hong Kong. Because of Canada's close geographical proximity to the U.S., shared language, and similar regulations and legal system, it appears safer. Yet, there are many U.S. businesses selling successfully to other countries!

Those firms have not only realized the potential of foreign markets, including Asia, but more importantly, they know what's needed to take advantage of those opportunities. Careful planning and locating the right assistance, including state export promotion agencies, can open up countless opportunities.

If you really want things to work in your favor, develop your GEE network. The Global Entrepreneurship Ecosystem (GEE) refers to your network of key contacts that assist you in your international sales growth.

This network may encompass international trade groups on social networking platforms such as LinkedIn, your local World Trade Center, SME development centers, your local Chamber of Commerce, the U.S. Commercial Service, collaboration with a reputable university, your state's office of international trade, or similar resources.

It's important to consider exporting, regardless of the size of your business.

CHAPTER THREE

WHY SHOULD YOU EXPORT?

With barriers to trade falling and trade activities growing at unprecedented rates, the domestic market is getting extremely competitive, especially due to incoming foreign players. To tackle this competition, businesses need to simultaneously explore other markets for their products and services while competing better in their local markets. The U.S. market makes up only 5% of the world's consumers. Not tapping into the remaining 95% of the global market is a huge loss for any business. Even if you're benefiting from regional growth, diversifying your client base by entering new foreign markets is well worth the effort.

Despite current uncertainties associated with the global COVID-19 pandemic, the World Bank forecasts the global economy will reach $72 trillion by 2030, with exports from the U.S. growing by 10% every year. Your products or services can easily be a part of this growth, which is being largely fueled by consumers in India, China, and other growing economies. The global market is an incredible revenue torrent for businesses of all sizes in the U.S.

Small business owners often ask themselves why someone from another country would buy their products. Surprisingly, among successful exporting businesses, few of them have marketed unique and amazing products. Rather, the majority of businesses began with everyday products, but relied on superior marketing and customer service. They were passionate about expanding globally, had solid business fundamentals, and knew how to close a deal. One such business that calls itself "micro-multinational" has only 40 employees, but sells to approximately 60 countries.

Entering the global market broadens the vision of the company and adds to the skills and knowledge of everyone working in that company. There's an automatic transformational effect on all members of the organization, expanding their knowledge of the world economy and helping develop relations on an international scale, all of which opens up more opportunities. Expanding a business globally takes time and commitment, but once it becomes established, a business is poised to experience rapid growth and improved professional efficiencies. At this point, you are heading in the right direction.

Learning about other cultures and identifying their needs, figuring out how to meet those needs, forming new relationships, and addressing new business challenges result in improvements in processes as well as the products or services themselves, which in turn makes them more competitive in every market. Moreover, addressing the needs of a diverse customer base is highly rewarding.

If your product or service previously sold well in the U.S., but is losing market share to more tech-savvy products, a sizable export market may still exist. This is because consumers in other countries may not be able to afford expensive high-tech products or may not need state-of-the-art technology. In many cases, it takes years for the latest and most sophisticated technology to reach the Third World countries. Hence, you shouldn't abandon an export strategy just because sales of a product are declining in the U.S.

At the same time, if you decide not to expand beyond international boundaries, you increase the risk of diminishing sales for your business. Simply put, with the ease of selling internationally today, it's highly likely that your competitors have already started selling abroad or will enter the market very soon. They'll be able to enjoy all the benefits of exporting mentioned above, leaving you further behind the competition. Businesses that fail to capitalize on the benefits of exporting will find it harder to keep pace with new ideas, technology and product improvements. Exporters receive a tremendous amount of support from state entities because they contribute to the state's economy. Your growing competitors will benefit from government assistance and free trade agreements, making them less likely to fail, regardless of their size.

Therefore, even though 58% of U.S. exporters sell to only a single foreign market, i.e. Canada, there are numerous small U.S. ventures selling to more countries than the number of their employees in their organization! They are the ones experiencing skyrocketing sales growth, as the major portion of their revenue comes from foreign markets. You can very well be among these "mini-multinationals."

CHAPTER FOUR

DEVELOP AN EXPORT STRATEGY

LICENSING AND REGULATIONS

The first question that comes to mind for anyone considering exporting is whether they need an export license. While all export items are subject to U.S. government regulations and export control laws, over 95% of exported items do not require an export license. However, even if your items do not require an export license, that doesn't mean you can sell them to anyone in any location. The government's export control laws and regulations determine who you can sell your products to, and which countries you can export to.

For example, certain dual-use products that are applicable to both commercial and military contexts, and munitions products, are subject to the U.S. Export Administration Regulations (EAR). The EAR's Commerce Control List (CCL) specifies all the items subject to the EAR, assigning an Export Control Classification Number (ECCN) to each. If your product is not listed in the CCL, but falls under the jurisdiction of the U.S. Department of Commerce, it's classified as EAR99, which doesn't normally require an export license. A Bureau of Industry and Security (BIS) export license may be mandatory for an EAR99 product depending on the country you are exporting to, the end buyer, or even the end-use of the product.

These export licensing controls are important for U.S. national security, nuclear non-proliferation, foreign policy, crime control, anti-terrorism, and regional stability.

How to Ensure Compliance

One strategy for ensuring compliance is to set up an Export Management and Compliance Program (EMCP). This enables you to examine every piece of compliance-related information and analyze your export decisions in order to develop them into an integrated and well organized system.

Begin by visiting the BIS website (www.bis.doc.gov) and studying the 10 core elements of an EMCP. While exploring these elements, also study the EAR's record maintenance requirements.

If your product assortment comprises hundreds of items, make a written compliance plan. In addition to studying BIS's online publications and videos, consider attending specific export control and EAR seminars to stay informed of any new updates.

For training, contact your local U.S. Commercial Service office or simply visit the BIS website. You can also contact the BIS directly for guidance on devising a compliance plan and help with assessing the final plan.

Compliance Strategy

Your inventory management system must contain a field for classification information for each item. Create an additional field where you can add the specific licensing requirements for each product and the name of countries for which the EAR restricts export of that product.

Before adding a product to your assortment, ask your supplier(s) for the product's classification information and enter it into the relevant field. However, don't rely solely on the information your suppliers provide. Work closely with them to see how they have determined the ECCN number of each product. However, keep in mind that it's your responsibility for ensuring compliance for any product you export.

Your export documentation, such as the commercial invoice, must include the export classification and license numbers. The EAR also lists certain types of exports under section 758.1, for which you must file the respective electronic export information in the Automated Export System, regardless of the destination or value. Likewise, for certain EAR shipments, major freight carriers and the U.S. postal service typically require you to enter "NLR" (No License Required).

The importance of classification under the EAR cannot be overstated, considering that if your inventory management system does not have an ECCN or EAR99 designation for an item(s), then it is ineligible for export. Your inventory management system should be sophisticated enough to immediately flag any problematic orders, especially those subject to the EAR. You simply cannot afford to make mistakes when it comes to EAR compliance, no matter if your items are EAR99 or have ECCNs.

Arms Regulations Compliance

If you produce or sell defense items or services, you need to be particularly well versed about the International Traffic in Arms Regulations (ITAR), which controls the sale of these items.

To begin, refer to Part 121 of the ITAR to find out whether your product is included in the U.S. Munitions List (USML). If yes, you'll have to thoroughly research ITAR licensing on ITAR's official website. If you attempt to export any USML item without acquiring the necessary licensing, you'll put yourself in serious trouble.

Who Can't You Sell To?

Based on national security goals and U.S. foreign policy, you cannot sell to certain countries, companies, and individuals. The list of entities you cannot sell your products to is maintained by the U.S. Department of Treasury's Office of Foreign Assets Control (OFAC) and the BIS administer, who enforce trade and economic sanctions against these entities.

As an exporter, you must be aware of the countries, organizations, and individuals that are part of this list. You may even want to hire a third-party firm to monitor these obligations in real time on your behalf. Specialized software packages are also available to help manage compliance. While your freight forwarder may be able to flag any compliance errors, it's ultimately your responsibility to acquire the necessary licenses and meet all other compliance requirements.

YOUR PRODUCT'S EXPORT POTENTIAL

The next step after compliance is to determine your product's export potential. There are several ways to assess the export potential of your items in the international market. The domestic sales of your product are an obvious evaluator. If your product or service is performing well in the U.S. market, it is likely to succeed in foreign markets too, especially in regions with similar tastes and preferences. Assessing domestic sales is easy if you plan to represent a manufacturer or if you're a wholesaler yourself. It will give you a good sense of future prospects even if you plan to launch a startup.

In addition, examining your product features is another way to assess export potential. If the product features are unique in the overseas market and cannot be easily duplicated, the chances of product success are quite high. With little or no competition, the demand for the product is likely to be high in the global market.

However, this doesn't mean you should dismiss the idea of exporting if your product is not unique. Many items and services have competitors in external markets, yet they manage to make their mark through various tactics. For instance, sensible businesspeople position their products based on the dynamics of different markets. The same product sold with different USPs in different markets performs equally well. Likewise, sellers make use of other techniques that have little to do with the product itself, such as outstanding customer service. Sometimes, the mere fact that a product is "Made in the USA" is enough to attract foreign buyers. As explained earlier, sellers also benefit from information and contacts from the GEE and government assistance. Finally, fluctuations in foreign currency exchange rates and free trade agreements with countries can oftentimes make competitors' products more expensive, thereby helping American sellers increase their market share.

DEVISING AN EXPORT PLAN

While you should begin by setting goals and objectives and identifying constraints and capabilities, what's more important is that key management staff agrees on them. Meanwhile, other staff associated with export processing must also concur with every aspect of the export plan, since they will ultimately be responsible for the plan's execution and implementation.

The point of devising an export plan is to collate facts, goals, constraints, and prepare an action statement based on these items. When specifying the objectives, proper scheduling and marking milestones should be included so that measuring success is easy and keeps everyone motivated.

Be sure to include the following information in the export plan:
- The needs of the global marketplace related to your area of business;
- The products you plan to export and if any of them need to be modified or adapted to the overseas market;
- Whether you need an export license for any of the products;
- The targeted countries for export development;
- The basic customer profile of those customers in each targeted country;
- The best marketing and sales channels to be used for each targeted country;
- The potential challenges in each market, such as free trade restrictions, cultural differences, competition, etc,. and strategies to combat them;
- Various shipping costs, as these will determine the export price for products selected;
- The operational steps to be taken along with specific time frames;
- The schedule for the implementation of each element of the plan;

- The staff and resources that will be devoted to exporting;
- The cost of implementation for each element;
- The evaluation process and its effective use to alter the plan in the future;
- Any modifications in the packaging or labeling that might be required to adapt to the market of specific countries;
- Freight, import duties, taxes, and other costs;
- The procedure to protect your intellectual property, if required;
- Any modifications to your website that will help cater to the international audience, such as adding different language versions or a currency converter;
- Any other third-party e-commerce platforms you wish to sell on; and
- A social media marketing strategy

The first draft of an export plan won't necessarily be a lengthy document, since you aren't likely to possess substantial market data initially. As you start planning, obtaining more exporting insights, and identifying your competitive position in the overseas market, more information will be generated, resulting in a more detailed and complete plan.

If you intend to export directly to an end-user located outside of the U.S., a detailed export plan is still recommended. However, if you intend to export indirectly, such as through a third-party website, the plan can be fairly simple.

Regardless of how simple or detailed, your export plan should not be a static one. Instead, it should be flexible enough to undergo quick changes as you obtain more market information and insights over time. Also, the plan's objectives must be measurable with actual results to accurately assess your strategies.

Why Is It Important to Have an Export Plan?

Only one-third of the U.S. SMEs have a documented export plan. Most SMEs start exporting in response to a foreign order received via the Internet, and are likely to continue in this manner without exploring and creating opportunities for themselves. Without an export plan, these businesses go on without having any revenue targets or dedicated individuals for export development.

The absence of an export plan also contributes to SMEs overlooking lucrative opportunities. Not surprisingly, when you don't have an effective marketing strategy in the international arena and rely solely on a reactive approach, you won't receive many orders, which can be extremely demotivating for sellers. As a result, many SMEs shy away from exporting, believing that it's easier to serve local customers or that it's not worth the effort to sell to foreign customers.

Without an export plan, you tend to take exporting for granted. On the contrary, if you work hard to determine how to grow your global presence and increase exports, you will make better decisions about resource allocation and the overall business strategy, which increases the chances of success in the international market.

In addition, your strengths and weaknesses are more clearly expressed in written plans, making them harder to ignore or gloss over. Furthermore, it's possible that you will need to seek external sources of finance, which means you will need to present the plan when you approach institutions for funding.

Once you have a plan in writing, it becomes extremely easy to communicate it to others, for example, to new hires. Also, it makes it easier to assign duties to employees and track their performance. The clearly defined steps in an export plan assures a long-term commitment to exporting, keeping you consistent over time. Finally, since a written plan makes you better prepared for orders or product inquiries, you will be less likely to overlook them.

FACTORS TO CONSIDER WHEN MAKING THE EXPORT DECISION

Before entering the global market, the following factors must be considered and included in the export plan in order to avoid any issues, at any level.

Production Capacity

Look into the current production capacity and see whether it is being fully utilized. If yes, you will probably need to invest more to facilitate additional production. Your domestic sales should not be hurt in the process of fulfilling international orders. Identify the minimum order quantity required and how much cost will be incurred to enhance the production capacity. This will essentially depend on the specific design and packaging of the products produced for exports. Before commencing the production of export products, it is also important to track any fluctuations in the existing annual workload and take them into account while planning the production capacity.

Financial Capacity

The company's current financial capacity is another important consideration. You'll need to find out what financial resources can be committed to the marketing and production of the export items. This should also help determine the need for external funding, such as from banks. Once you have set aside an amount for exporting, you'll need to allocate it to the potential initial expenses. An expected date by which the export department should start paying for itself as well as the breakeven point should also be established. An ROI document is a commonly used document to set financial targets. Finally, find out if you qualify for export promotion assistance from the federal and/or state government or other entities.

Strategic Objectives

Upper management should be aware of, and support, any export venture. In addition, the objectives should be solid, such as a desire to expand the customer base to make it more stable or increase the sales revenue. Make sure a legitimate reason exists so as to avoid any negative outcomes.

Likewise, the commitment of the top management to exporting must be examined as well. If the sole purpose of exporting is to compensate for declining domestic sales, the management may start neglecting foreign customers when domestic sales pick up again. Also, management's expectation regarding how soon the export department should breakeven must clearly be documented so as to avoid any misunderstandings.

Allocation of Personnel

Before allocating personnel, you need to identify your company's existing in-house expertise to handle international clients, including language proficiencies and sales experiences. Once you have dedicated personnel for the export department, appoint a manager with responsibility for supervising and organizing the department's activities. Allocation of senior management and the resulting organizational structure should be clearly presented to help define clear responsibilities and hold people responsible for outcomes.

CHAPTER FIVE

CHANNELS IN THE GLOBAL SUPPLY CHAIN

When establishing a global supply chain, businesses must choose between adopting a direct or indirect selling approach in the international market.

Direct selling is when a producer deals directly with a foreign customer. Indirect selling is when a producer sells through an export intermediary, such as an export trading company (ETC) or an export management company (EMC). Many U.S. wholesalers work on this model, whereby the wholesaler buys goods from producers, then sells them to a foreign buyer, arranges for delivery, and receives payment. In this example, the ownership of the goods transfers to the wholesaler. The producer's responsibility ends at the point when items are sold to the wholesaler. However, the drawback for the producer is that they sell products at a lower profit margin than the wholesaler, who gets a higher profit margin when selling to international customers. This can create problems if a certain product doesn't sell in the international market.

A more feasible business model is a commissioned-based one in which the intermediary merely brings foreign buyers "to the table" and charges commissions to the producer on every sale. No transfer of product ownership takes place. Retail giants such as Amazon, Alibaba, and eBay all operate on a similar model. Their distribution facilities are strategically located in different parts of the world to serve international buyers, and they handle all paperwork, logistics, customs, and other functions on behalf of the sellers.

Deciding on whether to opt for a direct selling or indirect selling model depends upon the resources your business is willing to dedicate to exporting. Other than that, you need to consider the size of your business, the nature of items you plan to export, your shipment and order fulfillment capabilities, the amount of risk you're willing to bear, your expertise and experience in handling exports, the business environment and competition in targeted countries, the availability of resources for export development, and the opportunity costs of exporting.

There's not always a clear answer for which approach you should adopt. Based on the factors stated above, you can start with indirect selling and gradually go into direct selling as you gain more market insights, or use both methods together. Some sellers simultaneously sell to foreign buyers through their own website, sell on third-party e-commerce platforms, and sell through EMCs and agents who find buyers for them.

DIFFERENT APPROACHES TO GOING GLOBAL

The way you choose to "go global" will significantly impact your export plan and shape your marketing strategy. The various approaches to take your business to a global level vary in terms of your business's involvement in the export process. Let's go through each of them individually.

Selling Through Domestic Buyers

For the original seller, this method is no different from domestic sales. They sell to domestic parties who have identified the product's potential in the foreign market and take responsibility for handling all exporting and the associated risks. Many sellers don't even realize that someone else is selling their products abroad because a high demand exists for their products in the international market. Surprisingly, the majority of exporters don't manufacture the products themselves. They acquire them from producers, many of whom haven't even thought about going global. Some companies are aware of the soaring demand for their products in the global marketplace, and they produce products for export, but don't actually export themselves.

Selling to Domestic Entities
Representing Foreign Customers

Numerous entities represent a large pool of foreign buyers and purchase goods from local sellers to fulfill demand from foreign buyers. These entities include local and foreign enterprises, general contractors, foreign government agencies and trading companies, retailers, and foreign distributors. Again, the original seller usually knows that its products will be exported, but is not prepared or unwilling to bear the risks and additional operations involved in exporting. They rely on one or more of the above mentioned entities, which constitute a large market for various commodities.

Selling Through Intermediaries

This approach involves availing the services of an intermediary that can find foreign customers for your products or services. This approach differs from the above two approaches in that the original seller retains considerable control over the overseas selling process. There's also a high level of transparency. In fact, the seller also benefits from access to in-depth information about foreign competitors, advanced technologies, and new market opportunities.

As explained earlier, e-commerce platforms are one of the intermediary types that not only provide a global platform to sell items in exchange for a commission, but also offer shipment and handling for a specified fee. The e-commerce company collects payment from customers on your behalf and passes it to you according to a pre-defined payment cycle.

Direct Exporting

Selling directly to foreign end-users is the most rewarding, yet challenging approach. From planning to market research and distribution to the collection of payments, every aspect of the exporting process is handled by the original seller. If a seller really wants to achieve success in the international market, they can't take exporting for granted. To accomplish desirable results, significant time and resource commitment are required. That is why this approach is regarded as the most rewarding one, and can result in skyrocketing growth and maximum profitability.

Fortunately, this option is no longer confined to large corporate giants. Because the exporting process is easier than ever today, small and medium-sized enterprises are successfully exporting. Yet, proper guidance and help is key. The U.S. Department of Commerce, shipping companies, state trade offices, international banks, freight forwarders, and others offer guidance and resources to help businesses "go global."

Direct exporting comes with multiple options. For instance, you can start selling to international customers through your website, if you have one with a credit card payment gateway. The franchising business model also falls under direct exporting, but then you'll have to find and support a reliable, master franchisee. In addition, you can undertake direct exporting through a contract received from the U.S. or foreign government. This provides the seller with an opportunity to build up more contacts and boost their sales in the international arena.

Despite the benefits associated with the direct exporting approach, most U.S. businesses rely on the first two indirect approaches, neither of which requires active involvement by the original seller. Nonetheless, if the exports continue to increases in the future, they won't be attributed to the original sellers, depriving them of any export promoting grants or assistance from the government or any other entity.

Since this eBook aims to define how you can build up your global supply chain, I'll focus on the last two approaches to going global.

Indirect exporting may be appropriate for your business depending upon the availability of resources and the level of commitment you can provide. All you need to do is find an intermediary to handle exporting on your behalf. But, keep in mind that working with an intermediary or an EMC doesn't preclude the possibility of direct exporting. For example, you may choose to engage an intermediary for selling to high-risk Asian countries, while considering direct exporting to Canada and Mexico. As you gain more experience and increasing revenues, you can then start engaging directly with other countries. This is the most commonly adopted approach, and has helped sellers increase their international sales over their domestic sales.

It is also recommended that you seek guidance from the U.S. Commercial Service or other trade specialists before adopting a particular approach or choosing to use a mix of different methods.

DISTRIBUTION CONSIDERATIONS FOR DIRECT EXPORTING

When building your global supply chain, make sure you plan for the following distribution considerations:

- The distribution channels to use to market your products or services abroad;
- The location of the production site and how it aligns with foreign distribution;
- The possibility of establishing a production site abroad near the target market; and
- The availability of warehouse facilities in the foreign market to ensure a faster delivery to end-users, reduced freight costs, and a shorter supply chain

By getting directly involved in the export process, you can have greater control over the operations, attain a closer relationship with the overseas market and customers, benefit from technology and information inflow, and thus improve your company's competitiveness and profitability.

However, as opposed to the domestic market, the global market demands more complex functions. To support these functions, your business must undergo significant internal organizational changes. Before you begin direct exporting, you will have to choose the international markets to penetrate, and opt for the right distribution channels for each of those markets. It's only after these decisions are made that you can start building up connections and buyers in the overseas market to sell your product or service.

NECESSARY ORGANIZATIONAL CHANGES

When you start exporting, you'll normally proceed with the same organizational structure and personnel that you had previously. You must respond to emerging exporting needs and separate the management of your company's exports from that of the domestic sales as international sales and inquires increase.

As mentioned earlier, the global market is characterized by more complex functions that require more specialized skills. Apart from this, success on the international level requires a focused marketing effort. Both of these functions can be efficiently deployed by separating the international business from the domestic one.

However, you should know exactly when to separate the two divisions. If you segment too early, the company's resource allocation may become inefficient, while you might lose considerable export business if the separation occurs too late.

One option is to start with a plan in place, then as exports begin to multiply, you can proceed with segmentation, appointing dedicated resources for domestic and international divisions. You may also choose to have a separate export department right from the start, with a permanent or part-time export manage- who reports to the existing head of the domestic division. As the international business picks up, more autonomy can be given to the export department, which will start reporting directly to the business owner.

The key to achieving exporting success is your company's marketing efforts. Even if you lack an ideal organizational structure, focused marketing skills can help companies prosper in unfamiliar markets. Based on real life insights, when it comes to operating in global markets, the marketing methods used are more important than the unique attributes of the product or service being sold.

DIFFERENT CHANNELS OF DISTRIBUTION

Once you've organized your company to manage the export process, you now have to select an appropriate distribution channel for each market. Let's explore the five main distribution channels.

Sales Representatives

A sales representative operates as your company's representative, and uses your product samples and literature for business development in a specific overseas market. They are normally specialized in handling complementary products that don't conflict, and usually work under contract for specified periods, earn commissions from sales, and assume no responsibility or risk for your products or services. Some sales representatives work exclusively for certain sellers, while others work for several different clients. The contract for work with sales representatives includes the region, terms of sale, payment method, procedure and reasons for contract termination, along with several other details.

Representatives or Agents

Agents or representatives are individuals authorized by you to make commitments on behalf of your company in specific international markets. You should clearly state in the contract that the agent or representative has the legal authority to conduct business operations on your company's behalf. It is important to note that the word "agent" is widely misunderstood nowadays, as it seems to obligate the need for a power of attorney, which is not necessarily required for an agent or representative in this scenario.

Foreign Distributors

Foreign distributors are merchants you sell your products to, and who resell them to dealers or retailers in a specific foreign market for a profit. They are the most consistent channel for which to produce the desired results in overseas markets, particularly for small business exporters. The benefit of using this supply chain channel is that the foreign distributor provides service and support to the customers in that market, relieving you of that important responsibility. The foreign distributors are able to do this by storing sufficient product quantities in inventory, efficiently managing the supply of spare parts, and maintaining adequate staff and facilities for servicing operations in the respective market. They typically handle noncompeting, complementary items and do not sell directly to end-users.

Wholesalers form an important part of this channel. They resell to retailers in their territories. However, the challenge with wholesalers or other major distributors is that they typically will not engage with a small company with an undersized production unit, or with products that aren't expensive enough to earn big margins for the wholesaler.

Again, a proper contract is signed between the seller and the foreign distributor to define the length and terms of the engagement. A common approach is to begin with a short-term contract and keep extending it if the association proves beneficial for both parties. To search for and choose authentic distributors, get help from the U.S. Commercial Service, which can also provide guidance on structuring agreements. The complex labor laws in certain countries can impact your ability to terminate contracts. There are always rules and issues specific to different markets. Therefore, it is highly recommended to seek expert legal advice regarding the market for which the agreement will be in force. This also helps you understand your options in the event of a dispute. For instance, whether arbitration is a possibility, or whether you'll be able to conduct a trial in U.S. court rather than in a foreign court.

Foreign Retailers

Selling directly to foreign retailers is another option, but they don't necessarily sell complementary products. The products they deal in are limited to consumer lines. New opportunities are emerging for this type of direct sales, such as the growth of major retail chains in Canada and Japan. While this channel is mostly dependent on traveling representatives, the use of product brochures, mailing catalogs, and other literature can also help achieve the objectives.

By using the direct mail approach, you not only save on commissions paid to representatives and traveling expenses, but you can also reach a broader audience. However, this approach should be accompanied by other marketing activities for optimal results.

Many large U.S. retailers have overseas offices. If you're able to establish ties with them, you might be able to benefit from this relationship. For example, they might agree to sell your products abroad through their foreign offices.

But again, foreign retailers or resellers are more inclined towards established and well known brands. If you're a small company, they'll either ignore your proposals, or agree to work with you without promoting your brand as much as they would push large brands. Even if your products have great market potential, resellers can prioritize other products over yours simply because they receive higher commissions on those products. Furthermore, new exporters are often exploited by resellers who negotiate rigorously and maintain much larger margins than the exporter.

Direct Selling to End-Users

While this method was impractical for most businesses years ago, even the smallest business can now sell to end-users in another country without having to travel. End-users can be the final consumers, foreign businesses, or even foreign government institutions. You may also reach out to potential buyers via the overseas posts of the U.S. Commercial Service, international publications or trade shows. If you manage search engine marketing strategies efficiently through keyword auctions, purchase online ads, or use other tactics, potential buyers might reach out to you.

It's important to keep in mind that selling directly to end-users means that you will have to handle shipping, service operations, payment collections and every other aspect of an international sale yourself. Make sure to account for all these costs when setting your pricing strategy. If you fail to take into account any of these costs, you'll possibly make smaller profits or perhaps encounter losses.

If you prefer to use foreign representatives, domestic and international trade shows are the best places to find them. You might need to travel in order to properly identify, assess, and sign up foreign representatives that are right for your needs. In addition, conducting background research in advance can save a lot of time.

Aside from these channels, you also have the option to consider joint ventures and direct investments.

If you don't wish to leave the U.S. at all, the best and most effective method is to consider selling through e-commerce platforms. Also, you can conduct market research through the U.S. Commercial Service, which can help reach buyers in over 125 countries.

Importer of Record (IOR)

One of the most popular channels adopted by exporters these days is the Importer of Record (IOR). An IOR operates as an owner, purchaser or customs broker for products imported into a destination country. Typically, a power of attorney (POA) is used by the actual importer of goods to authorize the IOR to carry out the customs clearance on behalf of the importer. The IOR will ensure that all the imported goods are properly documented and valued, and that all of the import tariffs, duties and fees are paid. Among the most important roles of an IOR is to ensure proper compliance with statutes and regulations, usually through various compliance tools, which may include compliance software. The reason why the IOR becomes the responsible party for compliance, payment of tariffs, and other aspects is that this entity becomes the temporary owner of the imported goods until the goods are accepted at the distribution center.

An example of this is my own organization, Global4PL. Global4PL's IOR program helps U.S.-based sellers export their non-revenue international shipments to overseas markets without paying the duties and taxes associated with a Temporary Import License. In addition to minimizing your costs in foreign countries, the service presents a simplified shipment clearance process with an easily accessible document control system, and shipment tracking from all over the world. More importantly, it offers an export/import system that's fully compliant with all U.S. foreign trade laws.

HOW TO CONTACT AND ASSESS DISTRIBUTORS OR FOREIGN REPRESENTATIVES

Once you have a list of potential foreign representatives and distributors, send a personalized email or fax to each of them individually. Foreign representatives or distributors are constantly looking for foreign companies to work with. You will need to share your company profile and product information with the representatives. Oftentimes, they'll request more information about your company and the products you sell. Provide full information on your company's history, product line, resources, personnel, past export activity, and all relevant details. If possible, try to include some photographs of products and production plants, and ship some product samples, too. However, avoid sending product samples if there is a danger of intellectual property theft in your target market(s). If feasible, invite the foreign representative to visit and explore your company's operations.

Be sure to request ample information from the representative and vet them carefully before signing any contract. Here is a list of information you should request from foreign representatives:

- Their history and current status, including background on previous work;

- The approach used by them to introduce new products in the targeted region;
- Bank and trade references; and
- Information on how they can meet your company's requirements

Once you are satisfied with the above information shared by the representative, request that they share an assessment of the region's market potential for your products. Aside from providing valuable market insight, this lets you know how much knowledge the representative has regarding your industry.

You may choose to obtain feedback from business associates working with the representatives, but don't hesitate to ask questions directly from the representatives as well. Businesses certainly have the right to check the credibility of someone representing them in another country. Well qualified individuals won't be reluctant to disclose information about their credentials. On the contrary, they will be proud to talk about their qualifications and experience. Also, make sure to utilize official government offices to carry out background checks about the potential business partner before agreeing on a deal.

Alternatively, you can try and obtain at least two business and credit reports to verify whether the representative is reputable or not. To obtain more information, consider getting the second report from a different source. You can find reports for a number of representatives from the U.S. Commercial Service International Service Profiles or commercial companies. Commercial banks and firms are also reputable sources for credit information pertaining to overseas representatives.

Suppose you have a list of potential representatives in a particular country and you have obtained considerable business and credit information for each of them. If possible, take the time to visit the country and explore the size, location, and condition of the warehouses and offices. Meet the sales team and evaluate their strength in the industry. If visiting each representative is not feasible, set up meetings at trade shows held in the U.S. or another country. The U.S. Commercial Service can help tremendously in this regard. The agency not only arranges meetings, but also offers video conferencing facilities so you don't have to travel to a specific country.

SIGNING AGREEMENTS WITH DISTRIBUTORS OR FOREIGN REPRESENTATIVES

Once you've identified the ins and outs of a foreign representative and settled on your choice, you will need to negotiate a foreign sales agreement with them. Consult the U.S. Commercial Service or the International Chamber of Commerce before signing this agreement.

Most foreign representatives are interested in the following aspects and will negotiate accordingly:

- The profit potential of your product or service and their pricing structure;
- The payment terms;
- Support offered by you in terms of sales aids, advertising, and promotion materials;
- The amount of training you will provide to the sales and service staff;
- Information about your competitors and their share of the market;
- The regulations pertaining to the product; and
- Your firm's ability to deliver products on schedule

Typically, a foreign sales agreement will include terms requiring the representative to abide by the following regulations:

- Not partnering with competing companies;
- Not disclosing any confidential company information that can prove detrimental, injurious or even competitive to your company; and
- Informing you of any inquiries received from regions outside of the sales territory for which the representative is responsible

More importantly, the agreement must include terms requiring the representative to do their best to increase sales of your product in their sales territory for the compensation specified in the agreement. For this purpose, you will need to add performance metrics, such as the expected rate of sales increase and minimum sales targets for specified periods.

It is important to decide whether you should use the term "agent" for the representative when drafting the agreement. The problem is that in some countries, the term "agent" is used to refer to the power of attorney, which makes a big difference. Regardless of whether you use the term in the agreement, it is strongly advised to clearly specify whether the representative or agent has power of attorney or not.

Another important consideration is what language should be used to draft the agreement. Most agreements are drafted in English as well as the language of the sales territory.

Not surprisingly, foreign representatives normally request inclusion of an exclusivity term that states that you won't authorize any other party to represent you in the sales territory. Never agree to this when you are entering into an agreement for the first time. Let the other party prove their capabilities in the sales territory before making such a commitment. Another option is to include the exclusivity term for a limited, or a specified period, such as one year, which can always be renewed afterward. When including an exclusivity clause, don't forget to define the sales territory for which it applies to keep things as flexible as possible.

The foreign sales agreement must also specify which law applies to the agreement. While you should definitely include this clause, keep in mind that the law of the targeted country can still take precedence over that which is defined in the agreement. To resolve contract disputes, most businesses include the United Nations Convention on Contracts for the International Sale of Goods. Others turn to international arbitration for contract dispute resolution.

Contract Termination

One of the most important things to include in the foreign sales agreement is the escape clause in case the representative cannot meet your expectations. The terms relating to contract termination allow you to end the partnership cleanly and safely in the event that the representative proves incapable. You can specify that either party can end the agreement by issuing a written notice in advance, clearly defining the notice period in the agreement. Also, the reasons justifying a termination can also be defined and included in the agreement, e.g."not meeting the predefined sales targets." Some businesses choose to limit the agreement to a year with automatic renewal unless one of the parties issues a written notice to end the contract.

No matter what termination terms you include, they must abide by the corporate laws enforced by the targeted country. Therefore, hiring specialized legal counsel is recommended when drafting the agreement. This helps you understand the corporate laws in the representative's country. Consider the following legal aspects associated with contract termination:

- The duration of the notice period. That is, how early in advance should you notify the representative of your decision to terminate the contract? Most countries' laws require at least three months, providing that a written letter was issued before the start of the notice period.
- The list of "just causes" allowing for termination of the agreement. This actually strengthens your position rather than weakens it, allowing you to end the agreement cleanly and safely with the representative, if required.
- The law that applies to resolving contract disputes.
- The method to calculate the compensation due to the representative at the time of termination. This isn't just based on the sales made by the representative, but also takes into account the business development they conducted for your products and services in the country, as well as the "just cause" used for termination. The representative will normally have to be compensated for losses incurred due to these aspects and for any value they added to your business.
- In the event of contract termination, the representative must return any property, trademarks, patents, customer records, and name registrations. Look for these aspects in the legislation, as you will definitely want to include them in the agreement.

SHIPPING
KG
24

CHAPTER SIX

SHIPPING

Having a well maintained e-commerce website isn't enough to execute a direct exporting program. You have to have an efficient supply chain to ensure that the products are delivered timely to buyers in all global regions. When it comes to shipping items overseas, a multitude of additional functions are involved, including packing, documentation, labeling, regulatory compliance, and insurance requirements, to name a few.

Proper packaging/packing is important to ensure that the product reaches the customer in proper condition with an accurate piece count. Correct labeling is equally important to make sure the product reaches the right destination and buyer. Insurance is mandatory so that you are compensated for any loss or damage that occurs during the shipping process. In addition, both the U.S. and the destination country have documentation requirements that must be met for the maintenance of records and reporting, along with collection standards.

All of these requirements can be overwhelming for businesses, which is why many freight forwarders offer assistance to perform these types of services.

ASSISTANCE FROM FREIGHT FORWARDERS

Freight forwarders are licensed agents that handle cargo shipments, both domestically and internationally. Typically, the international freight forwarders are well aware of the specific rules and regulations applicable in other countries, as well as the documentation requirements for various destinations. They help tremendously in calculating the overall costs, including their own freight charges, port costs, documentation fees, consular fees, and insurance costs, among others. They even provide expert advice on the best packing methods, as well as offering packing services, including special containers, if necessary. Details on all of these items will be required to set the pricing strategy for products sold overseas.

Another critical service provided by freight forwarders is reviewing all documents when the orders are ready to be shipped. Oftentimes, they make arrangements with overseas customs brokers so that overseas documentation requirements are met. This ensures that the products do not encounter any entry or admissibility issues upon arrival in the destination country. Note that while it is helpful to avail these services from freight forwarders, there are other options. For instance, many freight forwarding giants, such as United Parcel Service (UPS), DHL, and FedEx, are also customs brokers.

SHIPMENT REQUIREMENTS

Packing

International shipments are subject to certain packing requirements that vary from one country to another. When preparing a package for export, four major problems can arise, including breakage, pilferage, excess weight, and moisture. If your buyer shares packaging requirements specific to the port system in their country, make sure you follow them strictly. If they don't share any specific requirements, follow these standard packaging guidelines to avoid any issues:

- Use robust containers with appropriate filling and sealing as required;
- Regardless of the container size, the weight inside should be evenly distributed to provide proper bracing;
- Keep products on pallets and use moisture resistant material;
- Avoid writing brand names or contents on packages to prevent pilferage;
- Use safeguarding material to wrap the goods, such as seals, shrink wrap, and straps;
- Follow any product-specific packaging requirements;
- Verify compliance with all documentation requirements and markings for chemical treatment and fumigation

Private leasing companies and carriers also provide containers for international shipping that vary in size, structure, and material. While these containers are best suited for standard package shapes and sizes, they will accommodate most cargo. Liquid bulk and refrigerated containers may also be available. Some trailers are simply semi-trailers, which are transported via truck-tractor to/ from the port of lading and the destination port.

Air shipments are typically lighter in weight than ocean shipments, yet they should also be adequately packaged to avoid pilferage. Depending on the location, you may simply use domestic packaging if there are no concerns about damage to the contents or the display packaging.

The weight and volume of the packages are key to determining the cost of transportation. To minimize these two elements while ensuring sufficient protection while exporting, specially reinforced and lightweight packing materials are available. If you aren't equipped to render proper yet inexpensive packaging, hire a professional company to do this for you. The fees are moderate, but the cost savings can be significant.

Labeling

Markings and labeling are important when exporting containers and shipping cartons for compliance with shipping requirements, to facilitate proper handling, hide the contents, make shipment identification easier, and ensure compliance with safety and environmental standards.

The export marks required for containers and cartons should be specified by the overseas buyer so they can easily identify them upon arrival. In addition to the shipper's mark, you typically need to indicate the country of origin, package weight, handling marks, cautionary markings, ingredients, the port of entry, indications of hazardous materials, and the number of packages and the size of each.

Documentation

One of the most crucial aspects of managing the global supply chain is the documentation process. It is highly recommended to have a freight forwarder handle the documentation process for you. They are specialists in export and import documentation. You may have general knowledge of the documentation process, but it can vary significantly depending on a specific transaction and/or product. Both the requirement for the U.S. government and that of the destination country can be different for various transactions.

Minor omissions or discrepancies in documentation may potentially prevent the export, or result in payment issues or seizure of your goods by the foreign customs agency or U.S. Customs and Border Protection. While you are the responsible party for complete documentation, this is routine work for freight forwarders, who are less likely to make mistakes.

Different import regulations are in place for different countries. The shipment destination determines the number and various kinds of documents that are required. Exporters should utilize the assistance of their local U.S. Commercial Service to obtain the most up-to-date documentation information for the country to which they plan to export.

Here are some documents that exporters commonly deal with:
- **Airway Bill**

  This is a non-negotiable document required for all airfreight shipments.

- **Commercial Invoice**

  This is simply the bill for the products being sold, and sent by the exporter to the buyer. This document is often used by governments to determine the true value of a shipment in order to assess customs duties. You will need to follow the invoice format specified by the specific foreign government, which will also state the number of copies that need to be included. Other requirements, such as the language to be used, should also be provided and must be followed.

- **Consular Invoice**
  Some countries also require the consular invoice, which includes information about the consignor, the consignee, the value of the shipment, and the description of the goods. The customs officials in these countries use this document to verify the quantity, value, and type of shipment.

- **Bill of Lading**
  This is the contract between the owner of the package(s)/goods, and the carrier. Two types of bills are applicable for shipment by vessel: the straight bill of lading, and the negotiable bill of lading. While the former is non-negotiable and the ownership of the goods does not transfer, the latter can be traded while the goods are in transit. To take ownership of goods, the customer needs the original bill of lading that proves ownership.

- **Certificate of Free Sale**
  While this document is not required by every country for every type of good, you can obtain it from your state government. The document simply indicates that the goods you are intending to export have been previously sold in that state.

- **Inspection Certification**
  Some countries or buyers require this certification to check the credibility of product specifications. Normally,

an independent third-party organization performs this inspection.

- **Certificate of Origin**
This is a signed document verifying the origin of the goods being exported. Regardless of whether the commercial invoice contains this information, some countries require this document. The reason is that this document is validated by a semi-official organization, for instance, the local chamber of commerce.

- **USMCA Certificate of Origin**
The United States-Mexico-Canada Agreement (USMCA) replaced the North American Free Trade Agreement (NAFTA) on July 1, 2020. The difference between NAFTA and USMCA is negligible for most companies as the main changes are mostly targeted to protect farmers, and to update laws in the digital era, environmental protections, and protections for biologic drugs. USMCA is operationally the same as NAFTA and should not present any problems for most exporters.

Like NAFTA, the USMCA provides duty-free treatment for "originating goods" from the United States, Mexico, and Canada. Under the USMCA, a valid certificate of origin must be on file at the time of claim for preferential treatment, which must be completed by either the Exporter, the Producer, or the Importer.

If the goods you are exporting are USMCA-qualified and you wish to claim zero-duty preference due to this qualification, you will need to present a USMCA certification of origin. This document is only applicable when exporting goods to one of the signatory countries of the United States-Mexico-Canada Agreement (USMCA), that is, to Canada and Mexico.

NOTE: Per U.S. Customs and Border Protection (CBP), the U.S.–Mexico–Canada Agreement (USMCA) does not require a specific Certificate of Origin, as did the North American Free Trade Agreement. Therefore, CBP Form 434 is not mandatory under the USMCA. For more information on preparing a USMCA certification of origin, see https://www. cbp.gov/trade/priority-issues/trade-agreements/free-trade-agreements/USMCA

- **Certificate of Conformity**

    Similar to an inspection certification, this certificate involves product testing by a third-party organization. An authorized organization will test or analyze the goods and issue the certificate. This document is required for only certain types of manufactured goods, and only by some countries.

- **Electronic Export Information**

    This is an important documentation requirement on the U.S. government's part, and is key to compiling U.S. export statistics. If the export items exceed US$2,500 in value, the exporter, the freight forwarder, or a qualified third party designated by the exporter, must electronically file the Electronic Export Information (EEI) document. Also, if the export goods require an export license or are sold to a restricted country or end-user, again the exporter must file the EEI document, regardless of the value of the goods. The regulatory agency for this document is the U.S. Census Bureau's Foreign Trade division. Exporters can file the EEI free of charge by visiting the AESDirect platform.

- **Dock/Warehouse Receipt**

  When the domestic carrier moves the export item(s) to the port of embarkation or the export shipping line, the dock/warehouse receipt is used for the transfer of accountability.

- **Destination Control Statement**

  This statement appears on the bill of lading or the airway bill as well as on the commercial invoice to inform the carrier and all foreign entities that the goods are subject to U.S. export controls and cannot be diverted according to U.S. law.

- **Insurance Certificate**

  This document assures the consignee that in an event of damage to the cargo during transit, the insurance will pay for the loss.

- **Export Packing List**

  This is a detailed document that lists all the items in each package and states the type of packaging used, such as a crate, carton, drum, or box. Moreover, the individual gross, net, and tare weights and measurements, in both U.S. and metric systems for each package, must also be included in this list. To make identification easier, package markings must be accompanied by references. The export packing list is used by the forwarding agent or the shipper to calculate the total weight and volume of the shipment and ensure that the correct cargo is being shipped. The document may also be used by the U.S. and foreign customs officials for various reasons.

- **Export License**

  This document authorizes the sale of certain items to specific countries. As discussed earlier, this document may only be required under special circumstances or for certain goods, like ammunition. Also, it depends on the destination of the export item. An export license may be required for all or most exports to a particular country.

Shipping

For international shipping, the standard information on a bill of lading must include the export marks that specify the carrier name and the latest arrival date at the port of export. You should also include the instructions to be given to the international freight forwarder by the inland carrier over the phone. Consider learning the method of international shipping through consultation with a freight forwarder. You may also want to arrange a booking contract, or a reservation of space before the shipment date. This can be extremely useful as carriers are mostly used for bulky and large shipments.

A common practice is to use the bill of lading under a multimodal contract for international shipments. This means that the responsibility and charge for the entire movement from the factory to the final destination is assumed by the multimodal transit operator.

When deciding on a method of international shipping, be sure to take into account the cost of shipment, the foreign buyer's accessibility to the shipped product, and the delivery schedule. Certain factors may provide you with an edge over other exporters. For instance, you can use a domestic airport rather than a coastal seaport to take advantage of lower domestic shipping costs and quicker delivery times.

In addition, some buyers want the products to be shipped to a free port or a free trade zone so they can avoid paying import duties. Therefore, don't forget to discuss with your buyer the details concerning the destination of the shipment.

Insurance for Shipments

Shipment insurance is important for the protection of sellers and becomes even more important when exporting. When in transit, your exported goods may be subject to rough handling by carriers, poor weather conditions, and other non-controllable hazards, which makes purchasing insurance mandatory.

When it comes to shipment insurance, two types of insurance are available: cargo insurance, and export credit insurance. Cargo insurance pertains to the shipment itself, and in normal circumstances, your freight forwarder or shipper will take care of this through a contract with an insurance company. Nonetheless, you still bear the ultimate responsibility. Export credit insurance, on the other hand, has to do with insurance against nonpayment. For example, your payment may be at risk in the case of default by the buyer, a foreign currency disaster, or political problems. To protect yourself from these risks, the buyer's lender and other financial entities included in your sales terms require export credit insurance to cover risks associated with nonpayment. Let's take a look at the two insurance types in detail.

Cargo Insurance

When the terms of sale hold you responsible for insurance, as stated earlier, you can secure export cargo insurance through a freight forwarder for a fee. Another way is to obtain your own insurance policy. It is advised that you choose either of the two options even if the terms of sale hold the foreign buyer responsible for the goods. You should not trust the buyer and assume that adequate coverage has been obtained. In the case of an unforeseen event, your company will have to bear losses for damages caused to the products. Marine cargo insurance can be obtained for shipments by sea and/or air. You can also purchase insurance from the respective air carrier for air shipments.

While cargo insurance coverage applies to damage, loss, and delay in transit, carrier liability is often limited due to international agreements. Plus, this coverage differs considerably from domestic coverage. Ideally, exporters should consult a freight forwarder or international insurance carrier for expert advice. Coverage is normally settled at 110 percent of CIP (carriage and insurance paid to) or CIF (cost, insurance, freight). However, you can decide on different components with the buyer.

Export Credit Insurance

You might take things lightly in the case of domestic sales, but when it comes to exports, insurance against nonpayment becomes extremely important. Here are four primary benefits of export credit insurance for exporters:

1. The most obvious benefit is that it eliminates, or reduces, the risk of possible loss of sales revenue. Ninety to 100 percent of the commercial, political, currency conversion, protracted default, bankruptcy, or war risk can be

eliminated by working with the Export Import Bank (EXIM Bank) of the U.S.

2. Through export credit insurance, exporters can provide beneficial terms of credit to qualifying international buyers. For instance, if the international buyer is not able to obta n a loan from their lender due to the risk involved, the EXIM Bank, or the provider of the export credit insurance, will cover the risk, enabling the buyer's lender to extend credit. This allows buyers to obtain more insurance for impo-t shipments.

3. When a lender's line of credit is insured, the EXIM Bank's coverage turns the exporter's foreign account receivables into high-liquidity receivables due to the insurance by the U.S. government.

4. Wherever the EXIM Bank offers coverage, new market opportunities develop for the exporters.

Payment Policies and Terms for Insurance

The following are the various types of policy options available:

- Short-Term Insurance usually covers non-capital goods, raw materials, components, spare parts, and most services, but is only applicable for 180 days or less. The tenure can be extended up to 360 days for capital goods, large agricultural commodities, and consumer durables, through the insurance policies of the EXIM Bank. However, 50% of the product content should be U.S.-based.

- Medium-Term Insurance is available to international capital equipment buyers, covering at most 85% of the contract value and insuring goods valued at less than US$10 million.

- Single-Buyer Policy is the policy option that applies to one specific buyer. Rates vary with the type of international buyers, the tenor, and the risk associated with the buyer's nation.

- The Multi-buyer Policy provides coverage to eligible international buyers who are able to work on "open account" credit terms. Exporters who have a Small Business Administration (SBA) working capital loan or an EXIM Bank loan can avail a 25% discount on EXIM Bank's short-term multi-buyer export credit insurance. Express insurance, a product of EXIM Bank, comes with a policy quotation, a streamlined application, and buyer credit decisions up to US$300,000 in five or less working days.

Policies for Lenders

Financial institutions that support exporters can benefit from the insurance policies offered by the EXIM Bank. U.S. banks that open a Letter of Credit at the EXIM Bank to fund U.S. exports are protected by the EXIM Bank. If a foreign bank fails to reimburse or make payments, the Letter of Credit will provide 95 to 100% coverage for the non-payment.

The Financial Institution Buyer Credit is a policy protecting international buyers of U.S. exports for tenure of less than a year. For private sector buyers, the policy covers political risks at a rate of 100 percent and commercial risks at 90 percent.

Import Tariffs

While import tariffs will be paid by the international buyer in all circumstances, you need to know the tariff charged at a specific destination to evaluate the impact on your product cost. The amount an international buyer is willing to pay for your product will most certainly be influenced by the tariffs he will be required to pay for the importation, which will be incorporated into your product's final cost. To find out the applicable tariffs for various commodities in different countries, visit Export.gov and sign up in order to access this information.

There are inherent complexities with exporting. Aside from the various costs and risks involved, the documentation and other requirements can be a headache if you're a new exporter and don't know who to consult. By now, you've probably realized that the most valuable sources of information are the international shipping countries themselves, and freight forwarders. Freight forwarders no longer just ship your exports beyond international boundaries, they also help in managing documentation, payment collection from international buyers, and warehousing in overseas markets.

CHAPTER SEVEN

DIGITAL INTEGRATION: E-EXPORTING TECHNIQUES FOR GROWING BUSINESSES

In today's world, online resources and capabilities are key to building a global supply chain for your business. A variety of businesses, regardless of size, are taking advantage of the Internet to reach millions of buyers worldwide. The growth is reflected both in the B2B and B2C electronic commerce. The global reach of the Internet provides a cost effective means of marketing products and services around the world. At the same time, establishing a corporate website helps create an online transaction mechanism. Today's customers want more control, expanded choices, order tracking, the ability to obtain product-related information and more, all of which is possible through the Internet. Savvy sellers establish an online presence and manage a customer service interface to address all queries and orders. With different language versions available for websites, exporters can sell to non-English speaking consumers as well.

Simply put, electronic commerce (e-commerce) is the sale and purchase of products and services online. Contemporary e-commerce websites bring buyers, sellers and even vendors onto a single platform for sourcing, selling and purchasing activities.

WHY USE E-COMMERCE?

For small, medium or large businesses, e-commerce has proved itself as the gateway to entering the global marketplace. The Internet is accessible to more than a billion people around the world, offering an enormous customer base for any business that seeks to expand globally. Likewise, lucrative B2B business opportunities continue to open up. Through online marketing campaigns, businesses are able to market their products to countries and continents previously thought to be beyond their reach. Moreover, businesses looking for better quality and cheaper supplies to fulfill their internal manufacturing and other needs have a huge number of suppliers to choose from.

CHAPTER EIGHT

RECOMMENDATIONS AND INSIGHTS

1. Classification is the first step in the export process. If the Product Classification (HTS), ECCN, License Exception, etc. are incorrect, you will have issues. Very few people know how to classify correctly. Ask your freight forwarder, customs broker, or trusted consultant. If the classification is wrong, you will have problems from the start.

2. Exporting is like mastering any other skill—you need to start with the basics. When it comes to exporting, there are easier countries (Canada, Australia, and Singapore, for example) and there are more difficult countries, such as Brazil, India, and Russia. Some countries have very high duty rates (Brazil at 100% or more, for example) and there are some countries with very low or no duties for exports, such as Hong Kong. Take the time to understand precisely who pays for the duty and taxes for your exports. Don't risk losing your product and 100% of the duty on your first export.

   Start with the easy countries and build your experience from there—once you have done it a few times, then you will be much better prepared to ship to more difficult countries. Don't start exporting to the difficult countries first.

3. There are easy products (hard disk drives and laptops, for example) to export, and there are more difficult products to export, such as medical devices, medicine, and cosmetics, as these may require FDA clearance. Equivalent approvals are highly regulated in most countries to ensure safety of these types of products. Start with easy products first. Don't start exporting medical devices or other difficult products first, if you can avoid it.

4. You should check whether your overseas customers are present in the official government databases to make sure that you are not doing business with unreliable entities. This applies to all types of customers, such as contractors, companies, and individuals. This is called DPL (Denied Persons List) screening. Very few companies choose to conduct proper DPL screening, which puts them in very serious risk.

5. If you ship a product to Miami or any other major port in the U.S., and you know that the product is then going to be shipped overseas, it must be treated as an export. This means you owe the same level of due diligence as if you were directly exporting the product overseas.

   Suppose you ship to a reseller and you don't know who the end-user will be. When the product finally reaches the end customer who activates the license, such as a software license, you'll be able to know who the end-user is. If it's an overseas customer, you now owe the same level of due diligence as if you had directly exported the product overseas.

6. An employee with an A1 Visa working on key technologies/coding/encryption may need an Export License (the Deemed Export License) to work.

    Likewise, hiring interns, contractors, coders and others who are not U.S. citizens and/ or U.S. permanent residents (aka "green card" holders) without checking with your trade compliance team can be a problem. All of this falls under "Transfer of Knowledge," which is an export. For example, training a Russian in Palo Alto, California is akin to shipping the product to Russia.

7. If your company is a foreign company and you are exporting from the U.S., then U.S. laws apply to your company.

8. Shipping a U.S. product from an EU member-nation to Russia, for example, is much more challenging than shipping from the U.S. to Russia. This is because the exports will have to comply with EU law as well, which in some cases, is stricter than the U.S. law. Aside from the complexity involved in shipping U.S. items from one foreign location to another, if anything goes wrong, you might be questioned about the intent to ship from a foreign country. Hence, you'll have to implement stricter measures when shipping via another country.

9. Confidentiality is extremely important when exporting technology. This sector is much more heavily regulated than other types of products.

10. If you have separate departments for AP, AR, HR, engineering, operations, and sales, but do not have an export/Import trade consultant, you may not be exercising the due diligence expected of a company of your size.

11. Always ensure that you screen your financial transactions (wires, payments, transfer of funds) against the government databases even if the banks are in U.S.-friendly countries. For example, if you transfer funds to pay a vendor in France, your vendor may not be on the blacklist, but if their bank is, you'll end up losing your funds. The OFAC (U.S. Office of Foreign Assets Control) is very aggressive in ensuring that companies do not transact with blacklisted entities, and there are many banks on this list. OFAC will seize your money if you transfer any funds to these blacklisted banks.

12. Know your Incoterms (International Commercial Terms). Published by the International Chamber of Commerce, the Incoterms clearly define which party is the exporter, importer, and who pays for freight, duties, and taxes. They also assign responsibility for which party is liable to the government, or governments; whether you are legally taking responsibility for the product; and in case of loss, who can present a claim or who is taking the loss. If your sales, purchasing, operations, and shipping personnel don't know and understand the Incoterms, you will face serious compliance and financial issues.

13. Compliance is not an operational issue; compliance is a management issue. If management has not invested the time, resources, and funds to have the systems, training, and personnel to establish a rigorous compliance program, then management has failed their responsibilities. A true

compliance program requires three essential components: people, systems, and knowledge.

Don't cut corners when it comes to compliance. Inadequate compliance is expensive, and Uncle Sam is happy to collect money.

14. Know that OFAC is the most aggressive governmental office when it comes to going after export violations. The last thing you want is to have OFAC at your door. OFAC is masterful at collecting money from companies that have not spent the time or resources to comply fully with their export requirements.

15. If your company's products or services are related to high-tech, encryption, self-driving/autonomous vehicles and/or drones, you are subject to more export regulations than you probably know, and your company needs to understand them all. Penalties of up to US$300,000 per violation apply in this area.

16. Bring in consultants or expert resources to help your export team. Given their knowledge and experience, consultants can typically review and ensure that your company is compliant within a couple of days. The recommendations may take longer to implement, but you will be much better off paying US$200 to $450 per hour over the course of a few days rather than facing a $300,000 penalty for a violation.

17. Understand that your export becomes an import once it reaches the destination country. Make sure you know the import requirements that apply to your product. For

instance, you may be exporting correctly, but you may not be able to import if you don't have the import licensing or don't meet other requirements in the destination country.

18. Finally, if you never perform a post-audit of your export-related records and transactions, you cannot truthfully claim that your company has done its best to perform due diligence. This means you aren't doing the minimum to ensure compliance, which can put you in trouble. Therefore, organize regular post-audit programs, which are particularly important for compliance. Without it, you will not be able to identify violations in time. Committing an error or a violation one thousand times is equal to one thousand violations. Therefore, calculating your risk is easy: 1,000 X $300,000 = $3,000,000, plus a chance to be in the newspaper!

COMMON EXPORT MISTAKES

Some businesspeople begin exporting with difficult products. By difficult, I mean highly regulated products, such as medicines or medical equipment, food items, cosmetics, etc. The U.S. FDA, or its equivalent agency in other countries, has very specific and high-quality standards for these product categories. Therefore, if you're a small business or new to exporting, it's better to stay away from such products, as compliance with corresponding regulations can prove costly. If your core business relates to any of these product categories, you should already have a clear idea about the local regulatory standards. With a little more effort, you can obtain compliance information for your targeted countries. Nonetheless, if you're a startup or these products don't make up your core business, avoid starting with them in the international market.

1. **Starting With Difficult Countries**
   Similarly, when stepping into the international market, consider tapping into easier markets, such as Canada, Singapore, and Australia. Exporting is like a muscle—you begin by stepping onto the easier paths, learning the basics and achieving elementary growth. Over time, you move on to more difficult countries. Some inexperienced exporters choose to sell to difficult countries such as Brazil, Argentina, India, Indonesia and others that do not easily welcome imports. These countries carry hefty import

duties, which are a top consideration when potential buyers are negotiating product prices with you. Brazil, for instance, has an import duty of 100% of the CIF cost. Furthermore, a high level of payment insecurity exists in these countries. Unfortunately, there's a high risk of non-payment due to poor law-and-order. As a result, even the biggest global retailers won't fulfill orders in these countries unless payment is made in advance.

2. **Incorrect Perception About Exports**

   Some new exporters believe that exporting is all about "shipping a box" overseas. In reality, it's a much broader concept that includes the following additional exchanges:
   - Customers downloading software overseas;
   - Payments overseas for services;
   - Providing goods for demos;
   - Emailing specs/diagrams to a foreign vendor and/or customer; and
   - Hiring and giving access to coders overseas

Note: Hiring a non-U.S. citizen in the U.S. or abroad is considered an export—if you need an export license to export to that country, you may need an export license to hire the citizen of that country, even when he/she resides in the U.S. (this is called a "Deemed Export").

3. **Not Exercising the Import/Export Laws Despite Being Aware of Them**

   Having procedures and not following them is worse. It only opens the door for questioning your intent to circumvent the law. It is very important to respect all laws and comply with them.

4. **Not Treating a Free Sample as an Export**

   Some companies do not follow their normal export process when shipping non-revenue items, such as free samples. As a result, they face issues on every check point. If you ship a sample unit to an overseas customer for free, it's still regarded as an export. Keep in mind that every product that goes out of the country is an export—and is therefore subject to any and all export controls associated with shipments, transfers, and downloads.

5. **U.S. Product Sold Foreign-to-Foreign**

   Here's something that very few businesspeople know: every time a U.S. product is sold in any part of the world, it is regarded as a U.S. export. A shipment of U.S. technology from Germany to Hong Kong (for example) is a U.S. re-export and should follow the same level of compliance as shipping it from the U.S. to another country. Likewise, German export laws would apply as well in this example.

6. **Selling to CINSS via Another Country**

   As a U.S. exporter, you cannot sell to any of the CINSS countries—an acronym for Cuba, Iran, North Korea, Syria, and Sudan. As you might guess, you would also be violating U.S. laws if you were to sell to Cuba or any other CINSS country via a foreign country.

7. **Not Managing Proper Documentation**

   One of the most common exporting mistakes is not keeping records, or improper recordkeeping. Your freight forwarder (or FedEx, UPS, DHL, or TNT, for example) keeps the records for your shipment, but that doesn't necessarily ensure your compliance with applicable regulations. You cannot rely on freight forwarders, who typically maintain the records for only 3 to 6 months. If you try to access records a year later when the government demands, you aren't likely to access any. It is highly recommended that you manage the necessary documentation at all times so that you can provide them in a timely manner, particularly in case of emergency. You should retain your documentation for at least 5 years, and in some cases up to 8 years.

8. **Classifying Products on Their Own**
   Not everyone can classify products for exports, as most are not familiar with the Harmonized Tariff Schedule (HTS) and are inexperienced at classifying products. If you rely on past classifications for export products, you will likely end up having the wrong classification because classifications are subject to change. There is a reason why the government provides The Rules of Interpretations of Classifications. Therefore, you need an expert to perform the classification, and someone who is well versed in how the government writes regulations. Seeking professional help is the only sensible solution.

   It is also recommended that you maintain a product compliance database that is continually updated with any changes in classifications.

9. **Company's HR Doesn't Know That It's Also Responsible for Exports**
   It's pretty common for the company's HR department to know about A1 Visas. But oftentimes, they have no idea about export laws. That's not acceptable. The HR head and/or department should possess comprehensive knowledge of export/import laws.

10. **Relying on One Person For All Export/Import Compliance Needs**

    Most people possess knowledge in one area, but lack information in another. For instance, most people either know exporting or importing, but not many are experts at both. The same applies to domestic versus international shipping, with some people having knowledge of U.S. laws, but unfamiliar with foreign laws, which is not uncommon.

    Therefore, if your company relies on one person for all your international trade compliance needs, this presents a significant risk.

11. **Not Wanting to Know the Law**

    Not knowing the regulations is no excuse for non-compliance. Due diligence mandates that you should proactively find out if you have issues, while the government also tends to be more lenient if you correct those issues fully and proactively. Not checking because you are afraid to open a can of worms may jeopardize your ability to avoid penalties by taking advantage of Voluntary Self-Disclosures/Prior-Disclosure provisions.

    Even worse, it may place you on a Grossly Negligent rather than Negligent (or Fraud) list, because your company didn't even bother to learn about the regulations. If your company is big enough to have a finance department, then it should have a compliance program.

12. **Considering Compliance as a Cost Center**

    Compliance is not a cost center. It's a tool of efficiency. If your company can operate in multiple countries efficiently, you will have a competitive advantage over you-competition. Thus, don't see compliance as a cost center—see it as your efficiency weapon.

13. **Not Filing for CCATS**
CCATS (Commodity Classification Automated Tracking System) is an authorization in writing from the government, which guides you on who and where you can export. For some products, you are required to apply for a CCAT, while for others, it's voluntary. Many exporters ignore this entirely, putting themselves at considerable risk.

14. **Failing to Screen Customers and Orders Against the Denied Persons List (DPL)**
The U.S. government as well as its allied countries have developed extensive lists of companies, persons, and countries which you should not do business with, and which carries large monetary penalties for doing so. Additionally, you don't want to support these criminal, terrorists, or governments that support them.

15. **Neglecting to Ask For Help or Not Using Consultants**
I know consultants are expensive, there is no question about it. However, a consultant will be able prepare your company for success in a matter of days, while mitigating the risk of costly mistakes. The cost-benefit to incorporate years and years of experience into your venture in a couple of days will pay off handsomely.